Seven seas to sail

Welcome Aboard!

& seven notes to a scale.

Other Works by Mark Jager:

The Starboard Quest

Mystic Michigan Series

Mystic Michigander

The Hidden Hand

The Tell-Tale Earth

Zosma Publication

**Book Design by
Shaun Soper**
soper.design

The
Starboard Quest
TREASURE HUNT

In Search
of the Ladder

by Mark Jager

The constellation Lyra is depicted as a celestial harp with
the wings of an eagle and is found in the sign of Sagittarius.

Researchers have discovered that all of the objects in the
solar system are heading towards Lyra
at a rate of twelve miles per second.

Contents

FAITHFUL·IOHN

IT HAPPENED, AS THEY WERE STILL JOURNEYING ON THE OPEN SEA, THAT FAITHFUL IOHN, AS HE SAT IN THE FORE PART OF THE SHIP, & MADE MUSIC, CAUGHT SIGHT OF THREE RAVENS FLYING OVERHEAD. THEN HE STOPPED PLAYING & LISTENED TO WHAT THEY SAID TO ONE ANOTHER

SWAIN Sc

Introduction

How is it, that some of the most important beliefs the human race has had, can just disappear out of a sudden lack of interest? Beliefs which have been the central purpose of civilizations for centuries can vanish over night.

How are such crucial things erased from an entire society's memory in what seems like moments, when just a short time before that, people were willing to be martyred to preserve the cause?

Even in the proceedings of our everyday lives the questions run deep. How is it that we have very little curiosity about the founders of our civilization, and don't really have a speck of interest in hearing much of what that they had to say?

Nearly every day, we use the math, and the writing and reading skills they introduced to the world thousands of years ago. As far as more recent accomplishments given to us by our fore-bearers, we enjoy driving down the highways they designed, using the electricity they discovered, and think nothing of it as we pop our instant food products into microwave ovens they designed. However, we seldom have time to hear what they might have had to say, because, quite frankly, we find it boring. Is it that we think we are superior to those in the past? More intelligent?

Have we ever taken the time to consider the fact that there were multitudes of people who came before us, who lived their lives in service of others while trying to make the world a better place for those who would come after them? Does it ever occur to us, that there is a strong possibility that we should do the same?

Even on a larger cosmic scale, in things much more important than temporary things, the same mundane apathy seems to prevail.

People take a quick glance up at the star filled sky, and then look away…. unmoved. They know that it's a miracle that everything up there runs with precision clockwork, and has never lost a second in thousands of years. Yet, as people rush through their glance at the night sky, they yawn, and begin thinking about what they may have for dinner.

Have you ever considered it strange, that we know virtually nothing about the people who came before us? That we understand very little about those who shaped our whole modern reality? Also, isn't it odd that gaining information about these people is right at our fingertips through looking online, yet there are many people among our fellow citizens who won't even press a few buttons to read what they had to say?

I began to look, and to study what many of these sages had written. Many times, simple, yet absolutely amazing concepts were hidden behind an obscure intellectual vocabulary.

When a person presses on through the veil of intellectual code language, and begins to understand the simple concepts that hide there, an amazing way of looking at things is exposed. A literal treasure trove of ancient thought.

Many of the ideas in this book have been around for thousands of years. I'm just sharing what many other people have already written. You'll have to be the one to decide what you'll believe in this book. It's your decision.

The ideas set forth in this book are basically just reiterating things that have already been said. You may or may not choose to believe them, you will decide whether or not you're going to let them have any relevance for you. If nothing else, it's simply interesting to know how people in ancient cultures viewed the Earth and Universe.

So let's move forward now. Welcome aboard! It's time for a treasure hunt.

The Picture Story

In this brief moment of time, still the waves of your inner being. Focus your mind upon the thoughts that are presented to you on the pages of this book.

Do this in the hope, that the solution to a musical mystery will emerge from the depths of your inner being and find its way into your conscious mind.

Consider the implications of each sentence of this book. If you do this, it's message will be more easily mastered.

See to it that the thoughts presented in this book are clearly absorbed. A tool has been developed to help make sure this happens. What is this tool, and how will it help you retain the information in this book? The tool is mental imagery. Most people remember things if they have clear mental pictures of concepts created within their minds.

For the sake of mental clarity, you are about to be placed in an imaginary scenario by means of a picture story. Are you ready? Here it is.

Imagine while reading this book, you have climbed aboard a ship which is on a journey through time and space. The waves that this ship is sailing on, are SOUND waves. You are sailing on a sea of sound. Your purpose on this imaginary ship is to seek out, discover, and gather musical treasures scattered across innumerable islands and beneath the sea.

In this descriptive picture story, the island treasures are symbolic of the musical knowledge and epiphanies that lone individuals throughout history have written down.

Let's imagine the treasures at the bottom of the sea in this mental picture represent the musical revelations of humanity in general, they also represent that which will be discovered in the depths of your own consciousness that will be triggered by thoughts presented to you in this book.

In the following pages, use the figurative language written, to help aid your imagination on this auditory treasure hunt.

Each chapter in this book presents musical knowledge written down by various people throughout history. Each piece of information presented can be visualized as being both a jewel, and a clue which leads to the next step in the quest. All the jewels along the way are simply a small sampling of the vast treasure trove that awaits you at the end of the journey.

As we set sail to embark upon this voyage of sonic treasure seeking, we must first go back in our imaginations to a dawn beyond remembrance. Pay close attention to what is written. Time is fleeting. The universal tide is ever in motion, and you may never sail this way again. The Aquarian waters call you forward to your destiny. Be calm, take your time, and you will have smooth sailing.

Take a nautical pilgrimage into the depths of your own inner being which we will call your inner ocean. In the Captain's quarters at the helm of your spirit, can be found a compass and a navigator's map. The map is within you. On your spirit the whole musical history of the world is written. This map is something that is etched into the very fabric of your being. This invisible inner map unfolds into seven separate sections, each section is similar to the rung of a ladder. You consult your inner Navigator. You begin to climb that inner ladder of your internal being.

Submerged within you, is the lost world of the musical past. You can find information within yourself if you know where to look.

Starboard Quest

In addition to the information hidden within your inner self, there is also a wealth of information buried within the ocean of the entire human race. There, within the consciousness of mankind, is a hermetically sealed treasure chest of universal musical knowledge. You need only to tap that wisdom.

As we make the excursion within, we gather the timeless musical fortunes buried in the rare literature of forgotten storehouses of information. Let's glide the glassy sea of sound to that peculiar place in the remote past when symphonic purposes were yet unborn in the womb of the deep.

Long, long ago…….. there was silence…….

then, suddenly, cutting through the celestial sea of space, the silver spray of music washed ashore on the coasts of a hundred trillion worlds. There was a time when music was first heard. Think of what a wonderful experience that was for the first people who heard and experienced it. Since that time, the universal tide of music has been forever in an ebb and flow.

Let's sail deeper. We can do that by envisaging that as we travel through time on the figurative sea of sound waves, a message in a bottle, similar in appearance to an old alchemical bottle, comes drifting from afar towards the ship. As this bottle is fetched from the symphonic waters, something illuminating is discovered. In the bottle is a small emerald, and a silver scroll.

What is it? Directions to the larger treasure. The lone emerald being only a hint of a greater treasure to come. The bottle was set adrift in these waters by musical sages thousands of years ago in hopes that it would one day be found. The scroll is opened. Your eyes fall upon its timeless message, and this is what it says………

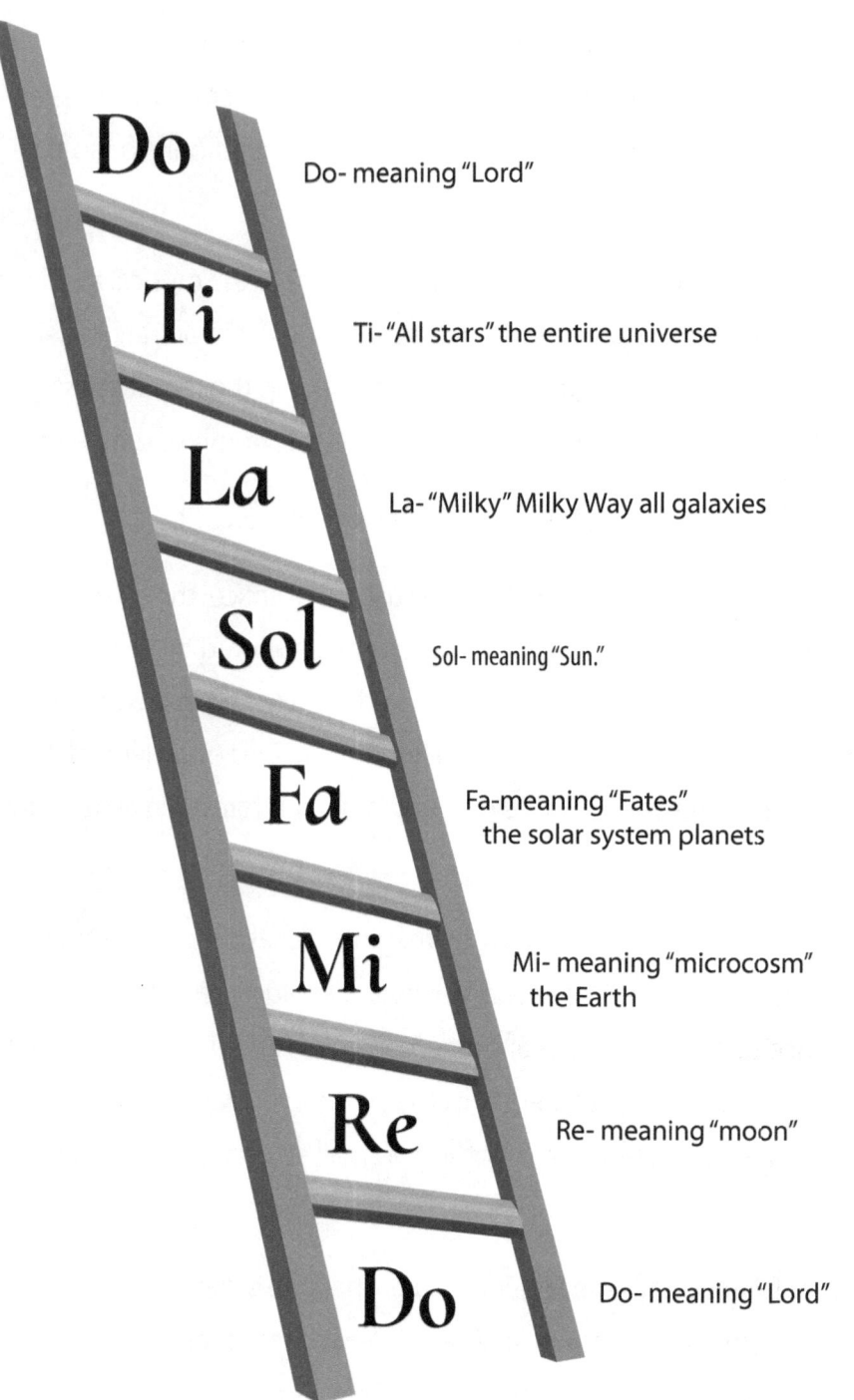

Do- meaning "Lord"

Ti- "All stars" the entire universe

La- "Milky" Milky Way all galaxies

Sol- meaning "Sun."

Fa-meaning "Fates"
the solar system planets

Mi- meaning "microcosm"
the Earth

Re- meaning "moon"

Do- meaning "Lord"

The word "octave" comes from the Latin word "octava dies" meaning "the eighth day."

The Ladder

As you open the scroll. You find the following words written with silver ink on golden parchment.

"Within and without,
to spirit from matter.
Climb the seven rung steps
of the pure golden ladder".

Now that you have been given a picture story to help create a mental vision of the age-old quest to discover the secrets of music, let's switch over to some real facts and real-life historical information. We will also examine the beliefs of ancient man. From time to time, we can return to imagery throughout the book.

In Greek, the word, "scale" as used in the words "music scale" means, "ladder". Therefore, when a music scale is mentioned, what is being spoken of is a musical ladder.

The following word picture is similar to how ancient people saw the music scale. Picture a seven runged golden ladder. Each rung on the ladder represents a note on the music scale. The lower notes on the ladder are representing the lower notes and as you ascend the ladder you are rising rung by rung to the higher notes.

A look into the meanings of the Latin names of the notes of the scale reveals something deeper.

Not only were the rungs on the ladder thought to represent the ascending notes of a musical scale, all the levels or rungs of the ladder were seen as a cosmological map representing the different levels of space and the levels of the spirit world a soul would have to climb up to ascend into heaven from the Earth.

It appears as if someone has left us a musical code. This secret cipher has been handed down from generation to generation by being preserved in a simple ascending musical scale we have all sung since childhood. Therefore, these notes are imbedded within humanity. Most likely this tune is known to most people in the world and crosses all cultural barriers. However, there is one problem with this nursery rhyme, whoever wrote it, must not have known what the Latin meanings of the words were. Other words were substituted. (Do, a deer etc.). So, although the actual ascending notes of the music scale are committed to memory, we grew up with a false understanding of what those words meant.

Where does the idea for this symbolic musical ladder or music scale come from? Who invented it? Textbooks will tell you the Idea for it came from the Greek philosopher Pythagoras. Further studies, however, will reveal that Pythagoras learned this music scale from Egyptian priests.

The Egyptian priests in turn, claimed that many of their musical ideas originated in pre-Pharaoh Egypt from a Monotheistic prophetic seer whom the Priests called, "Hermes Trismegistus".

The name Hermes Trismegistus is found in many places in ancient Egypt. His name was found inscribed on the Rosetta Stone when it was discovered in July of 1799 by French soldiers during Napoleon's invasion of Egypt. The Rosetta Stone has been on display in the British Museum since 1802.

The early Church Father, Clement from Alexandria said there were 42 books of Hermes. He mentions that there were quite a few different topics covered. Among them were books on astronomy, and the music of the gods.

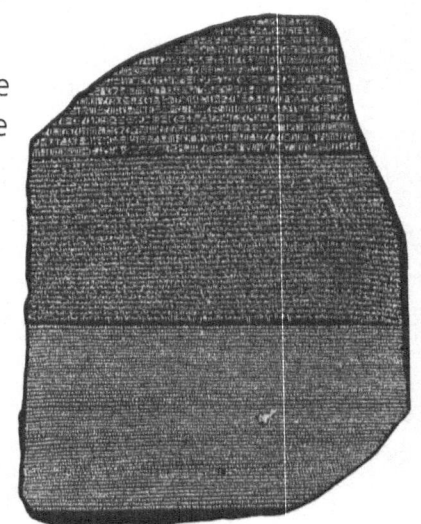

The Rosetta Stone

In addition to this, an assumed ancient writing called "The Corpus Hermeticum" was discovered near Alexandria, 132 miles north of the Great Pyramid. It is attributed to Hermes Trismegistus. In the book, Hermes mentions seven rings that a soul must ascend through to ascend into heaven. The same 7 rings had to be descended through for a soul to come to earth.

This ancient text speaks of the seven rings of 7 celestial bodies. The rings spoken of, represented the orbital paths of the celestial spheres of our solar system.

The rings are the outer perimeter of the orbits of 7 celestial bodies in our solar system. Each one of these rings can be likened to the rungs of a ladder. They referred to the sun and moon as planets. They assigned a music note to each of the seven spheres they knew of in our solar system.

Ancient man believed that as souls were coming down to Earth to become animated in physical matter, they would come down this ladder of planetary rings and come under the luminous influence and

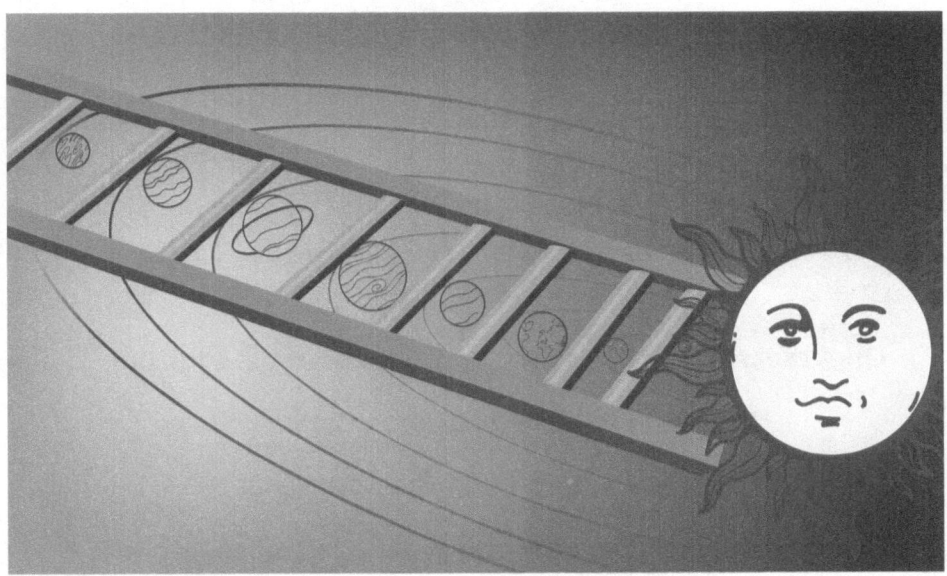

governorship of the various lustrous celestial bodies and the spiritual beings who oversaw them.

They would gain more and more strength in their souls as they came down through the rings. At the same time, part of them became more and more restricted.

This could be where the idea that planets were gods developed. The actual original ancient idea behind this, was that there were governing entities in charge of the planets. Those who arrived a number of years later seem to have gotten confused and began calling the planets themselves "gods."

As far as the ancient idea went, as souls came down this radiant ladder of planetary orbital rings on their way to being born, they would come under the influences of that particular governing agency or planet. Each planet had a different influence and power.

The soul would then acquire the benefits and strengths of that planet to equip them for their life on Earth. Yet at the same time, it would come under a type of necessary restriction from that planet. The soul became equipped to learn and gain the benefits of the exerted powers of that planet, yet at the same time it would come under the limitations of it.

Pythagoras is said to have given the blueprint for the structure of the soul. He believed that the soul was a symmetrical geometric reality. He believed the soul was possessive of 7 potent powers. He believed that each of these 7 inner soul energies were in harmony with and matched up to their own corresponding planets in the solar system. In other words, he believed that the planets were symbolic of processes going on in the soul. As the soul came down to Earth, the power of the Creator was coming through these planets to infuse certain qualities into this soul for human life. These were each specific powers which would be needed for the pilgrimage on Earth.

One researcher teaches that the 7 powers of the soul are;

> 1- the power to be rational - from Jupiter
>
> 2- the power to be emotional - from Venus
>
> 3- the power to be imaginative - from the moon
>
> 4- power to be intellectual - from Mercury
>
> 5- power to be contemplative - from Saturn
>
> 6- power to be dynamic - from Mars
>
> 7- vital powers - from the Sun

He believed the larger universe, beyond the solar system, consisting of the constellations, corresponded to and had a direct connection to the human spirit.

Then, finally, he seen that the four elements, earth, water, air, and fire corresponded to the actual physical body. The human body is in fact composed of earth, water, air, and fire (cosmic light).

There was a music note assigned to each planet The Greeks even assigned a mode to each constellation. The idea was that each musical mode or note influenced human beings in a certain way. These notes and music modes were supposed to be directly connected to the planetary modes or influences and were also directly connected to the 7 invisible powers of the soul mentioned above. Where all the stars and planets were located at the moment a person was born was believed to put an imprint on the body, soul, and spirit that would affect that person for their whole life. Each star or planet influenced that person. Directly connected to the stars and planets were the music modes.

For example, the Dorian mode was used for war. Ptolemy the Greek astronomer associated the Dorian music scale with the constellation Pisces. Greeks would compose music in this mode for their soldiers. When the soldiers came under that mode, they may have become more warlike.

Certain planets and constellations under certain conditions may have made people feel the same way. The planets may have produced the feelings and behavior of the music, and the music produced the feelings and behaviors that the planets did.

The belief in many cultures, was that each musical mode held a quality that would influence human beings to act a certain way.

Each planet had a musical mode that corresponded to it. To come under the influence of that planet, was to come under the influence of its "music".

If people were falling in love, they would most likely play a mode that was conducive to love. If they went to war, they'd play the music mode conducive to that. As far as individual planets Venus became associated with love, and Mars became associated with war.

In general, the idea was, that peoples' spirits or souls had something in the fabric or essence of them that could be affected by whatever powers were being radiated by the heavenly bodies. People became subject to these powers during their lives on Earth.

Then, when their lives were completed, the soul was thought to ascend back up above the planetary influences. The soul would retain all the good qualities that it had absorbed from the planetary spheres while living on Earth. At the same time, when the process was completed, the soul would be completely liberated from the planetary restrictions. Some believed the planets themselves were gods. Others, that the planets themselves were not the source of the power but were the distributing agencies of that power to man.

So, in a nutshell, in this way of thinking, elect souls were on this planet to obtain dynamic strengths and revelations that could only be obtained by coming here. A type of divine chemistry was being worked out through all the trials, tribulations, and other factors over the course of a lifetime. Situations were present in the great laboratory of the Earth to add all the right admixtures into the fabric of the elect souls.

There was a belief in a cosmic ladder of space. How much of a connection a human being was believed to have with that ladder, according to ancient beliefs may surprise you.

To find out more about this connection, you need to grab the next message in a bottle coming our way. Here it is now.

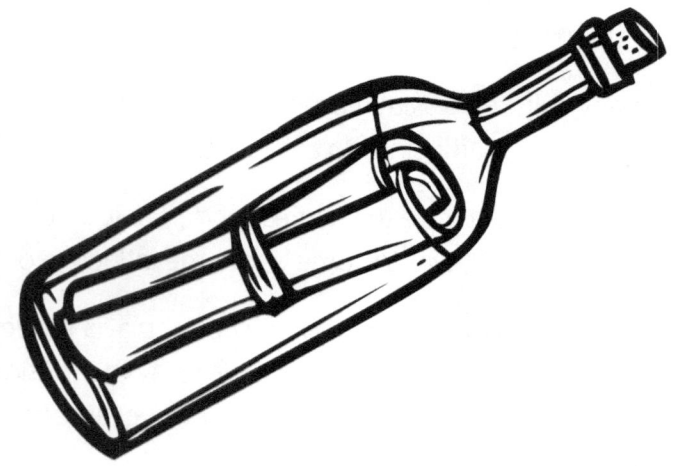

The Ladder Within

As you read the next clue, this is what it says,
"From octave to octave.
The beginning and the end.
You can climb to higher worlds on the ladder within".

The functions and components in the systems of the human body are amazingly comparable to the functions and components in the systems of outer space.

For example, the human body is made up of atoms. The electrons of an atom orbit around its nucleus in a similar manner to what planets in various solar systems orbit around suns. The Nucleus and electrons of atoms within the human body take on the appearance of miniature solar systems. (

A conglomerate of atoms work together in unity to form a human body. In a comparable way, planets and stars within solar systems work together to form the "body" of the universe.

Many people within ancient cultures viewed the universe as the body of Deity. They believed that just as a human body has an anatomy of various parts working together to form a whole, so did all the planets and stars work together to form a body.

The belief was that just as the human body is composed of atoms which operate like solar systems, so is the entirety of outer space formed of atoms which compose the body of the universe, which they named, "Universal Man".

Let's use the faculties of our imagination a moment here. If a human being was shrunk down to be many times smaller than an atom, and could observe atoms operating in a human body, the atoms would look like solar systems with planets orbiting suns. They would also appear to be operating in vast regions of empty space. This is because there is space inside of an atom, and space in between atoms. There is more empty space than there is matter.

Researchers say an average sized man is composed of 7 octillion atoms. That's a 7 with 27 zeros behind it. By comparison, researchers estimate that there are 200 billion-trillion stars in the universe.

So far, they have discovered 3,200 stars in the Milky Way galaxy alone that have planets orbiting around them. This would make it logical to conclude that there are at least that many solar systems in this galaxy.

In the human body there is more space than atoms. There is space inside of an atom, and space in between atoms. So therefore, the human body is composed of more empty space than it is of the mass of orbiting electrons and nucleuses. The same is true in outer space. There is more empty space in solar systems than there is mass of celestial spheres.

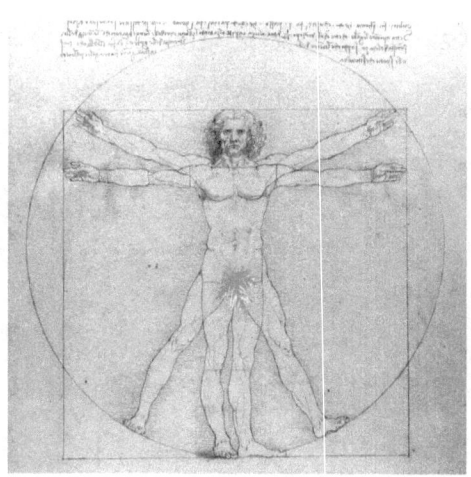

Leonardo Davinci drew his famous Virtruvian Man picture to demonstrate the connection between the human body, the Earth, and the universe.

Throughout history, researchers such as Leonardo Davinci have mapped out the anatomy of the human body and shown how it has its counterpart in the anatomy of outer space. In his drawing called,

"Vitruvian Man" Davinci demonstrated how the anatomy of the human body can represent the sacred geometry of both the Earth and the universe.

For centuries many people have believed that specific stars and constellations are connected to specific parts of the human body.

A good example of this type of belief can be seen In a diagram created in the 1500s by researcher Robert Fludd. These diagrams show various planets and constellations and what parts of the human body they were believed to be connected to.

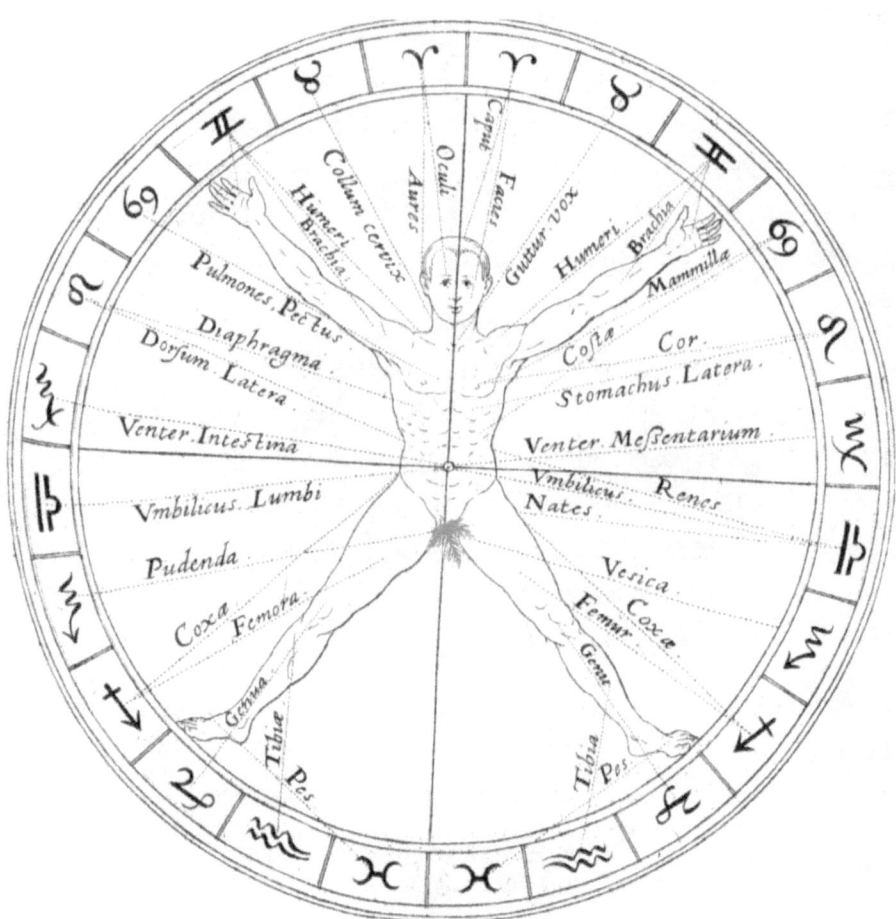

This picture, also from the 1500s depicts which specific heavenly bodies were believed to be in direct connection with certain parts of the human body

Throughout the centuries, researchers have viewed the human spine in a symbolic way. They seen the spine as a ladder that stretched from Earth to Heaven. This may seem like an unusual concept to people. One may wonder how someone could possibly come up with such a concept. Here is an explanation which will hopefully work out the details of this for the reader. Here is a view a bit different than Pythagoras's idea. The same type of concept is present though.

In several cultures, the stomach was emblematic of the earth region. The chest area was pictured to represent outer space. The head was regarded as being symbolic of the region of Heaven. The spine was a ladder that went up through all three regions.

There are 7 major organs of the human body: the lungs, liver, bladder, kidneys, heart, stomach, and intestines. In ancient thought, all these organs represented something on Earth or in outer space. Here are a few examples to convey the idea. The stomach, at the bottom of the spine, was viewed to be the bottom of the ladder. This was symbolic of the Earth itself.

As you climbed the ladder to the chest you were in the region corresponding to the planets. All the organs and parts of the chest mirrored things in space. For instance, the heart was viewed as a being a microcosm of the sun. All the blood cells in the body orbit through the heart. These could be pictured as being planets orbiting the sun. The circular system of the body which circulates the blood was likened to the circular orbital patterns of the planets in space.

The ladder reached all the way up into the head. They viewed the human head as the part of the cosmological map which represented the heavenly regions. They correlated the invisible powers of the mind such as mind, intellect, reason, and will, with Angelic principalities, powers, mights and dominions. In other words, the invisible powers of mind were, in the way they seen it, the direct correspondence of invisible angelic powers in heaven. These various parts of the human body were not only symbols of what was in space. In the ancient way of thinking, there was a direct connection between space and the living body.

Starboard Quest

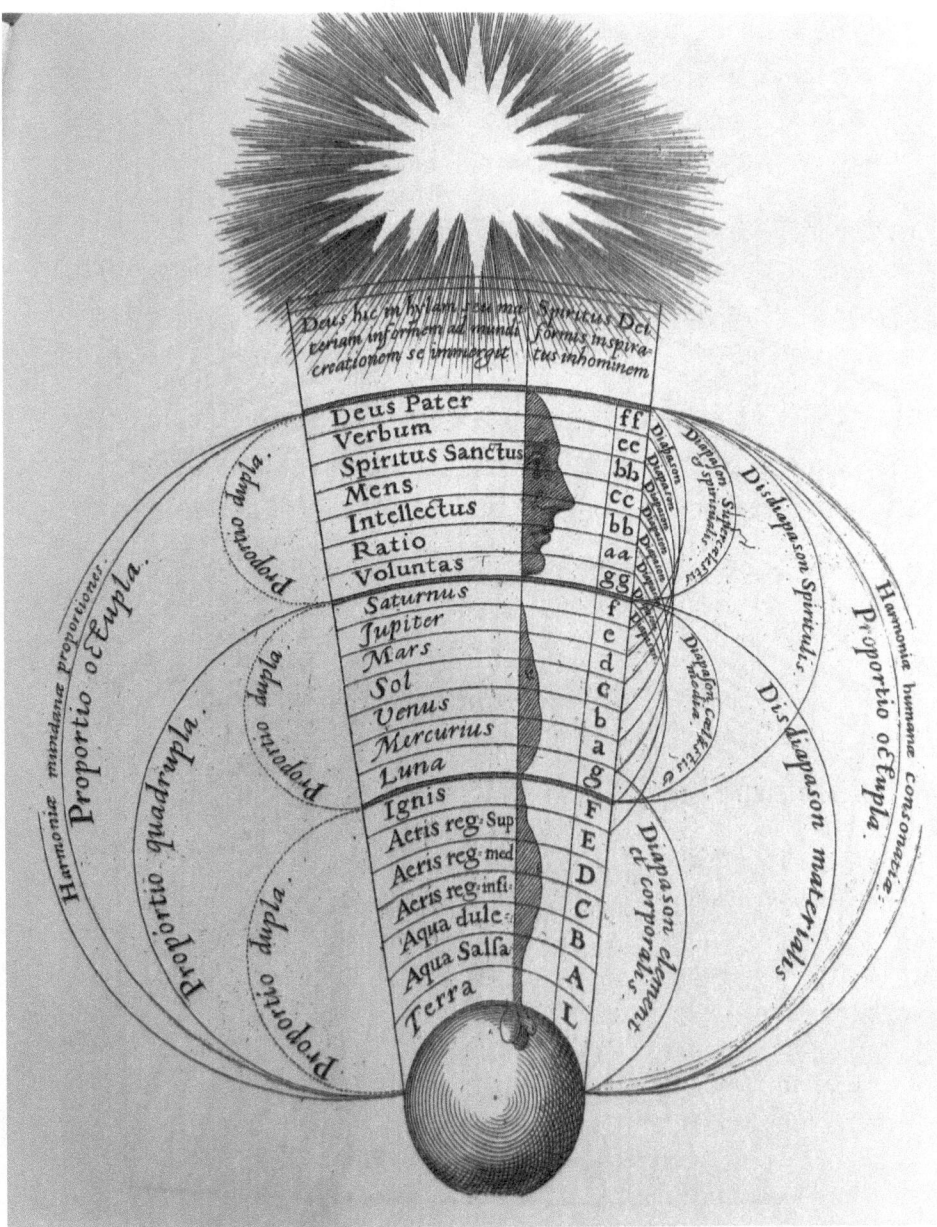

This diagram from the 1500s depicts the belief that the human stomach is connected to the Earth, the chest area to the solar system, and the head to the realm of spiritual beings and powers. The spine climbs up through all three regions like a ladder. The column at the far right shows the music notes that were correlated to each level of the human body.

As can be seen, the human body was thought to be directly connected with the universe. The human spine was viewed as an ascending music scale, a musical ladder that stretched from Earth to Heaven. Each level along the way represented an ascending musical note.

If a person studies the human spine, they will find something very interesting. It appears as if there can be a correspondence between the human spine and various music scales. This can be accomplished by viewing each vertebra as a note in a series of music scales.

Most people are born with 33 vertebrae. By the time they are adults the average person only has 24 vertebrae. Some of the vertebrae at the bottom of the spine fuse together during growth and development.

The spine is classified into three areas.

The lumbar vertebrae at the bottom, consisting of 5 vertebrae.

The next section up is the thoracic vertebrae consisting of 12 vertebrae.

The third section up at the top is the cervical vertebrae consisting of 7 vertebrae.

There are 3 very well-known music scales people use.

The 5 note pentatonic scale which corresponds to the 5 lumbar vertebrae.

The 12-note chromatic scale corresponding to the 12 thoracic vertebrae.

The 7 note heptatonic music scale corresponding to the 7 cervical vertebrae.

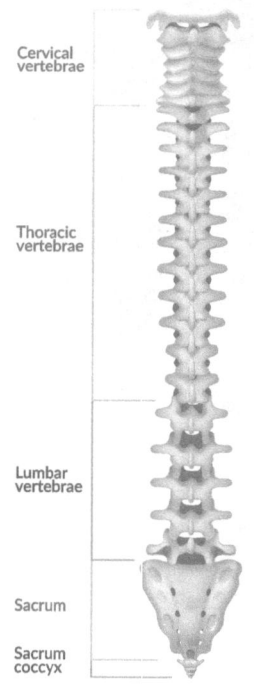

Cervical
vertebrae

Thoracic
vertebrae

Lumbar
vertebrae

Sacrum

Sacrum
coccyx

Correspondences between music and the anatomy of the human body are found everywhere. You probably couldn't write enough books to cover them all. This is just one example. Musical mathematics are found written right into the mathematics of our bodies.

Universal geometry can be seen in the human body too. Many have heard about the Fibonacci spiral. The spiral is a mathematical-geometrical spiral pattern that shows up in many places throughout creation. This pattern can be seen from the spiral of the Milky Way Galaxy to seashells to human fingerprints. The Fibonacci patterns from space are imprinted on the human body.

It is no surprise that it shows up in music as well. The keys of a piano are laid out in Fibonacci sequence, and there are even music notations that contain Fibonacci spirals.

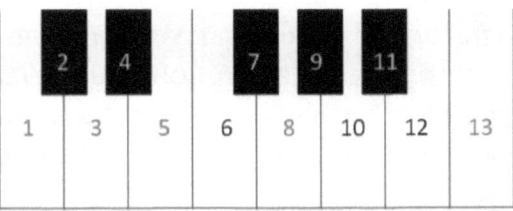

Before soundwaves can enter the human body they first have to pass through a golden spiral. Why is this? This is because the device gathering the sound waves is shaped like a golden spiral. This device is the human ear.

The diagram shows how the keys to a piano are laid out in Fibonacci sequence.

The Fibonacci spiral is directly connected to good acoustics. It is believed that the Greeks set up rooms in their buildings to have the best possible acoustics. Researchers believed they purposely set up the layout of these rooms according to the math of the Fibonacci spiral. Before they discovered this, the advanced knowledge of this acoustic design was already demonstrated in the proportions of the layout of the human ear.

Here is the process of how a human being hears sounds. First sound waves are collected by the golden spiral shaped ear. The sound waves are then channeled down the ear canal. They reach a sophisticated piece of "equipment" in your inner ear called "The organs of Corti" The organ of Corti contains miniature "harps" with somewhere around 15,500 strings made of tiny hairs. There are two sets of hairs in the harps. There are inner hair cells and outer hair cells. There are said to be 12,000 outer hair cells and 3,500 inner hair cells. It would not be surprising if there were 432x 36= 15,556 strings.

The sound waves strike the strings, the strings begin to vibrate. The sound waves are then converted into electro chemical signals and are sent to the brain. This is the most sensitive and incredible stereo system ever known to man.

Patterns within the human body parallel things that are in Heaven. There are patterns from outer space that are found in and upon the human body. There is a mini universe within mankind.

In addition to being a microcosm of the universe, the human body is also a microcosm of Planet Earth. How is this? The human body has creatures within its bloodstream and upon its surface. In fact, it is thought that there are more species of different types of life within and upon the human body than what there are creatures upon the face of the Earth and in all the oceans. Human beings radiate out heat from a core, just like the Earth.

In this way of thinking, human beings are a small-scale model of the earth, outer space, and heaven. Connecting all three of these levels is a ladder. This ladder can also be compared to a music scale. Symbolically speaking, you can climb to higher worlds by means of this inner ladder.

As the ship journeys on in its voyage across an ocean of sound waves, another message in a bottle appears to be glistening upon a distant horizon. Time to head in that direction.

PLATE LXI.

PROPITIOUS FORTUNE.

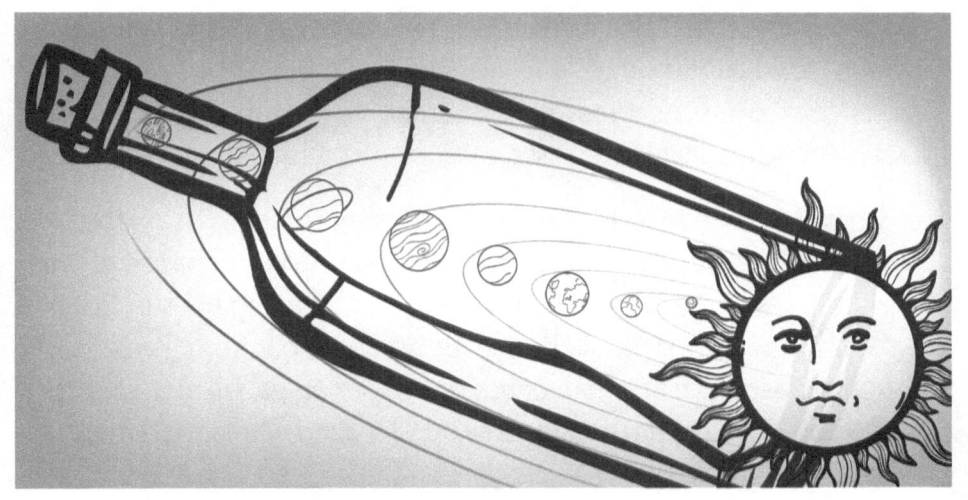

The Solar System
in A Bottle

Let's imagine that we are looking into the next clue that comes to us in our treasure hunt. The clue comes to us, like the others have, in the form of a message in a bottle.

Within the bottle, is a copper-colored scroll, and a zircon crystal. The scroll is taken out of the bottle and looked upon. The unrolling of the scroll has revealed a picture. The picture is of a man standing in the nucleus of an atom with all the electrons swirling around him. The picture is drawn in such a way that at the same time it can also be seen as a figure standing in a sun symbol with planets swirling around him.

Let's say that in a peculiar way that you can't quite put your finger on, the picture seems to be conveying the idea of transformation. It's as if the figure standing in the midst of the diagram is being changed by the electrons or planets whirling around it. There is no script to go along with the diagram. The picture speaks for itself.

Now, let's set aside this present imaginary picture story for a minute, and look at a belief from history that was accompanied by its own visual tool.

There have been people in ancient cultures who have imagined our solar system as being contained within a glass bottle. To them, the swirling planets in our solar system may have resembled elements being swirled in a solution contained within a glass beaker at a cosmic chemistry lab.

They viewed the circular orbital path of the planet Saturn as being the outline of a bottle. For if you were to draw out on a piece of paper, all the circular patterns of the planets in our solar system orbiting the sun, Saturn and the circle of its orbit would be the furthest orbit out from the center. So, if you were looking at a map of this drawn out on paper, all the other planets in our solar system would be swirling around within the larger circular orbit of Saturn which would contain them.

Perhaps an easier way to describe this would be, to imagine a circular shaped glass bottle, with a spout in the top with a cork in it. Then, in the very center of this bottle, imagine the sun. Then imagine the planets orbiting around the sun. The very furthest planet out from the center is the planet Saturn. Saturn is going around the very outer edge of the inside of the bottle, the furthest out from the center. Imagine the solar system spinning in a solution in a bottle.

What is the fluid they are being spiraled around in? A man named Franz Mesmer, may offer a clue through his discovery of magnetism. Interestingly, Mesmer was a friend of both Mozart and Haydn.

Mesmer had a unique way of looking at our solar system. Consider the following quote from Franz Mesmer concerning animal magnetism.

"There exists a mutual influence between the heavenly bodies, the Earth, and living bodies. A fluid universally diffused and continued, so as to admit no vacuum. Whose subtlety is beyond all comparison

An illustration of Franz Mesmer giving a treatment using magnetism technique.

and which, from its nature is capable of receiving, propagating, and communicating all the impressions of motion is the medium of this influence."

In other words, according to Mesmer, what we think of as being the atmosphere or empty space, is filled with invisible "fluid". An invisible, damp, metaphysical, substance surrounds the Earth and permeates the pageantry of all space. This invisible medium is called magnetism. It's an all-pervading essence.

The sun is the regulator of the magnetic fields of the glittering solar system. All things exist in a magnetic field. When solar explosions take place, such as when a supernova takes place, or when sunspots occur, the patterns of them can be seen in the rings of trees on Earth. The trees serve as antennas. They seem to allure into themselves the astral light which meanders down to the Earth as it makes its way down through the swirling whirlpools of the universe, and the twirling eddies of time and space.

There are magnetic fields on the Earth. Magnetic currents flow like ghostly waves across the planet. There are magnetic tides, with ebbs and flows. Human beings also have magnetic fields around their bodies. These magnetic fields are known as auras. Human bodies are literally enveloped in the vitality and exuberance of this timeless energy.

Theologian and Philosopher Thomas Aquinas is thought to have been one of the most influential thinkers of the Medieval period. He said that the magnetic fields of the human body were subject to magnetic tides. Albertus Magnus, who some have called the greatest German philosopher of the Middle Ages, said the human brain was subject to magnetism.

Thomas Aquinas

The planets and stars bombard the Earth with magnetism and energies of different kinds. For instance, the energy reflecting off the moon and onto the Earth, creates a different type of magnetism than what the sun does. Each type of light and magnetism has its own effulgence and are equally universally mesmerizing.

Certain flowers react to the moon and bloom at night. Other types of flowers bloom in sunlight. Chemical reactions in all living things take place throughout the world and it's all a reaction to the tides, forces, and powers of space.

Perhaps one of the best examples of a flower with a solar connection is the sunflower. A sunflower will raise its head up to the sun in the morning. It will turn its head during the course of the day to follow the path of the sun. In the evening, it will be facing the setting sun. When the sun sets, it will bow its head as if it were sad. The next morning it's facing east again as if to greet the morning sun.

A strong magnetic field protects the human body from infections, and contagion. All bacteria have magnetic fields. A weak magnetic field causes the body to be more susceptible to problems. We live in a sea of magnetism.

Magnetic fields of the Earth affect the fields of the body. Where is this magnetic energy coming from? The answer is, it's coming from outer space. At a deeper level, it's ultimately coming from the designer of space.

Plato said that the planet and its population have times of fertility and times of sterility. During times of sterility, there is a marked deterioration in human beings in many areas. It is said to affect health. It reportedly even affects creativity. At times of low magnetism, some researchers believe there are less artists and musicians. There's less creativity. It all has to do with space and magnetism.

The same report declares that during fertile times, vegetation flourishes as does human creativity. The flow of magnetism is thought to have something to do with the position of the zodiac signs. We are moving more fully into the age of Aquarius. This is the sign of the Man pouring out water into the mouth of the fish. What wonderful, wholesome, and nutritious stellar energies will be poured out in this age?

It's obvious the stars and planets work a procedure of chemistry on our bodies. To prove this, we only need to look as far as our food. We live off the energy from our food. All our food gets its energy from the sun, which is a star. So, we are basically consuming stellar energy that we have taken into our bodies through the food we eat.

All our cells which are orbiting through our circulatory system, and the atoms which are operating like miniature solar systems all get their energy for movement from space. Atoms are nourished by the same energy that feeds more than a Hundred trillion suns. Atoms are also exhibiting the same types of movements as Celestial bodies.

The tides of the Earth are affected by the moon. For years we've been hearing that more babies are born during the full moon. Certain animals are guided by the phases of the moon. The farmer's almanac even hints that the moon affects plant growth.

Some are of the opinion That during times of magnetic fertility, plants flourish. People become more creative, and it is all dependent upon the tidal forces of space.

Why all this talk of planetary energies and universal chemistry? What does the chemistry of the human body have to with space? What does all of this have to do with music?

Symbolically speaking, the universe resembles a huge alchemical kaleidoscope of sound and light. Let's go back to the solar system in a bottle idea a minute. The planets move around like various components and elements being stirred in a glass beaker, in a giant alchemical undertaking.

All the planetary elements evoke reactions from one another. They produce chemical reactions of gravity and magnetism upon each other. All this movement of the forces and energies affect the human race.

Mankind stands down on earth and the luminescent magnetism gracefully flows towards them from every direction. Human beings are being encompassed by celestial energy and music from every angle by a "stereo" that is presently beyond comprehension. Human beings are like the figure mentioned in the illustration mentioned earlier, which was depicted as a figure standing amid swirling atoms.

Ancient cultures believed that each star and planet was part of an extraterrestrial musical orchestra, an everlasting gyroscope of sound so to speak. Each orb exerts an influence and a magnetism.

Mathematicians have been proving for centuries that planets and suns are exhibiting musical ratios in their movements and in their sizes and distances from one another. Now, scientists all over the world are proving that many Celestial bodies are acting in the capacity of giant musical instruments.

Scientists at Sheffield University in the United Kingdom have released recordings of the sun making sounds. It is technically a musical instrument.

N.A.S.A. has recordings available for the public of music being made by every planet in our solar system. They have recorded impressions from plasma and transposed them into audible tones.

It has recently been discovered that the Earth's magnetosphere is acting as a musical instrument, and we are living in a massive magnetic musical instrument. The discoveries go on and on.

In summary, scientists are speaking in terms of planets being actual gigantic musical instruments. The entire universe and every creature and celestial body in it are reacting to the sounds and forces that these colossal instruments emit into the stellar fields. They produce cryptic and astonishing willo-wisps of sound.

The human body has shown evidence of patterning itself after the stellar macrocosm. Is it such a stretch then, to imagine that since every object in the heavens is affected by the music of the spheres, that our bodies, which composed of various types of stardust are too?

Consider this. The unseen mathematical, "musical" forces of stars and planets are causing chemical reactions upon the Earth, which is composed of earth, water, air, and fire.

Earthly music is also an unseen mathematical force. It's a force that has its roots in space. Our bodies are also composed of earth, water, air, and fire (electricity- and cosmic light). Is it beyond the realm of reason to speculate that we are going through a process of musical chemistry throughout our lives that involves sound and light?

Is there any evidence that ancient man tried to enact a galactic chemistry on himself while on Earth to assist him in his spiritual metamorphosis?

The Mirror of The Heavens

As always, a new message in a bottle has floated towards our ship. In the bottle is an azurite crystal and an iron-colored scroll. Upon its arrival, we take out the scroll, unroll it, and see that it is another picture. This is a picture of a looking glass which is reflecting the stars of the sky above.

The stars it is reflecting, are the stars contained in the constellation of Lyra, the celestial harp. It's handle contains engravings of sacred geometry, symbols of the zodiac, and the symbols of the sacred metals.

Sailing on now from this chapter's word picture, once again let's make the transition from symbolic word pictures to scientific fact.

Scientists have found that stars and planets emit frequencies. When the frequencies of stars are converted into sound waves and ran through a cymatics instrument, they produce geometric shapes and patterns.

Perhaps you haven't heard of cymatics or a cymatics instrument. Here's an explanation. Cymatics is the science of shaping matter with sound. A cymatics instrument consists of a flat square shaped box with a thickness of around three inches. On the top of this box is an inset metal plate.

A cymatics instrument

The cymatics instrument is set up in such a way that tones or frequencies can be sent through the box causing the metal plate on top to vibrate. When grains of sand are scattered upon the metal plate, and the plate is made to vibrate, the sand on top of the plate will arrange itself into different patterns depending upon what frequency is being sent through the box. This demonstrates that sound waves have an effect on matter. Some frequencies are thought to be healthy, good for the human body, and other frequencies are believed not to be.

Studies done on some of the Gothic Cathedrals have revealed that not only was the architecture splendid, but that the buildings themselves were designed to be finely tuned cymatics and acoustic instruments that magnified healthy cymatics frequencies and vibrations. There are patterns found engraved into the walls of cathedrals, that scientists are just now, realizing are cymatics patterns. Some of the designs for certain aspects of the buildings can be traced all the way back to ancient Egypt.

In fact, cymatics researchers have been amazed to find out, that when they do experiments in certain parts of the world, many times the cymatics patterns that emerge onto their plates take on the form of the ancient scripts from that part of the world.

For instance, a cymatics researcher was doing experiments in The Great Pyramid of Egypt. As he ran tones through his instrument, the shapes that appeared in the sand on his metal plate were in the form of ancient Egyptian hieroglyphics.

In fact, when he did an experiment in the King's chamber, he came up with a result that was enough to make the hair stand up on researchers' arms when they consulted ancient hieroglyphic experts and realized what it was.

Starboard Quest

One of the hieroglyphics that formed, was the double eye of God. Egyptian language experts confirmed that the hieroglyphic dated back in the hieroglyphic history of Egypt to a time before polytheism developed. The symbol traced all the way back to monotheistic times in Egypt and was deciphered to be the sign of "The Infinite One God".

The builders of the Gothic cathedrals utilized a unique combination of acoustics, cymatics, light waves, precision mathematics, sacred geometry, and symbolism. They also used building materials that would resonate with the human body in a healthy compatible way. When you think about it, these buildings can be likened to being a mirror of the zodiacal kaleidoscope above.

For example, at times red granite was used in the construction of many cathedrals. Sometimes they would travel great distances to get red granite, when other building materials were more readily available and closer to the construction site.

Red granite contains large amounts of quartz and iron. Quartz and iron are found in the human body. Quartz is found in the silica of human bones and iron is found in blood.

In fact, the human skull and blood are crystalline in structure just like a crystal in a radio receiver. Red granite is also similar in structure. So therefore, to construct cathedrals out of these materials is to construct buildings out of materials that resonate with the Earth's magnetic currents in the same way the human body does. Were cathedral builders trying to amplify the Earths magnetism?

Take into remembrance what Plato said about increased magnetism. He implied that human bodies were refreshed and flourished in a strong stream of magnetism.

Albert Einstein recognized that the human body is directly infused into the energies of the universe. He once was quoted as saying, "We are slowed down light and sound waves, a walking bundle of frequencies tuned into the cosmos."

In other words, the operations of the energy fields of our body are directly interfaced into the energy fields of the Earth and the powers of space. As has been said, the energy which fuels our bodies comes from food which has taken in sunlight. Which in turn is astral light.

In 2017, the Tokyo Institute of Technology discovered that quartz crystals at the Earth's core power it's magnetic field.

There are streams of magnetism that flow across this Earth at certain locations like rivers. It has been discovered that many of the Cathedrals across the world have been built right in these rivers of magnetism that flow across the Earth.

There were many hints of advanced learning placed in the construction and the symbology of the cathedrals. Many of the buildings were laid out with precision mathematics in their measurements. They were constructed according to the principals of sacred geometry.

In Ancient Greece for example, buildings were laid out in the golden proportion and fashioned according to stellar math. Solomon's temple was constructed in such a fashion that researchers say its acoustics were incredible. When researchers discovered the proportions that a concert hall should be built in, to be best suited for having excellent acoustics, it was pointed out that King Solomon's temple had already been built with the best acoustics possible thousands of years ago.

Sir Isaac Newton spent many years of his life studying the dimensions and measurements of Solomons temple and said that the temple was laid out in such a way as to be a map of the universe.

The builders of Gothic cathedrals constructed their buildings on Earth according to the patterns of things in the heavens. For example, in some of the buildings, on a certain day of the year, a beam of light would shine through an opening and illuminate a symbolic structure or symbol. Keep in mind, that stars emit certain frequencies. So therefore, that specific star, shining in at that angle, on that specific day, was bringing into the building a very specific frequency. It took astronomical knowledge to build a cathedral in this manner.

They had windows which were of various colors, that light would shine through. It has been discovered that certain colored light rays produce beneficial effects in people. Color therapy is a known field of study in the modern day. They had symbols and religious art. They burnt certain types of incense. It has recently been discovered that frankincense, an incense often used in religious services, has been shown to open certain areas of the brain that would normally be closed.

Everything was very finely attuned. What were they trying to accomplish? What affects were they trying to trigger within the participants taking part in the atmosphere that they had purposely created? Were they trying to put various factors together in such a way that it would create an atmosphere that would help prompt epiphanies in the observers?

Let's go back now to a word picture created in the last chapter. The symbol was the symbol of a figure standing in the center of an atom with mathematically precise electrons circling around him. The image symbolized transformation.

With that word picture in your mind, imagine that the person represented in the picture story represents a person sitting in the Gothic cathedral described above. The rays of light shining in on certain days of the year, the specific colors of light shining in, the specific frequencies coming into the building, the red granite, the acoustics, the incense, the sound waves, the symbols, all being like the electrons spinning around the figure in the picture story. Through the combination of all these different factors, was a certain chemistry being triggered in the minds of the people in the cathedral?

Perhaps a good illustration to explain the goal being aimed for in constructing an atmosphere in the cathedral like what was constructed, is a cyclotron. A cyclotron is an enclosed chamber in which matter is transformed by having atoms spun around it at great speeds.

Where does the idea of building sacred buildings on Earth which are mirrored from things in heaven come from? Many times, these buildings were made to be mirrors of astronomical things above.

Who came up with the idea of shining light through different colors of glass upon people? What was the inspiration for building sacred places on precise locations on the Earth? Who came up with the idea of placing sacred geometry in the structure of buildings? Who was the first to do this?

As was mentioned, Pythagoras is said to have had the knowledge of these types of things. He is also said to have had a vast knowledge of magnetism. However, the answer goes further back than him. Once again, we must go back to ancient Egypt for solutions. There we must meet the mysterious figure whom Egyptian priests called Hermes Trismegistus.

Upon the glassy sheen of the sea, a bottle sparkles in the incandescent moonlight. It's another message in a bottle.

A clue just surfaced. Time to open the next message in a bottle.

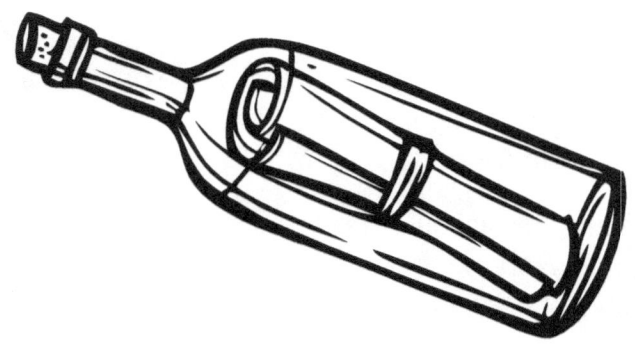

Hermes Trismegistus

The message in a bottle floats nearby. A small topaz is in the bottle along with the message. This is what it says,

"one man known by many names is the next clue".

Most of the musical knowledge we have today can be traced back to ancient Egypt. Pythagoras is often given credit for inventing the music scale as we know it in modern times.

As has been mentioned numerous times, Pythagoras spent many years studying in Egypt. It is thought that he received his knowledge of music and other arts and sciences from ancient priests in Egypt. The priests of Egypt, however, claimed that they had gotten their musical understanding from a mysterious historical figure named Hermes Trismegistus.

Hermes Trismegistus, depicted above, was known as the scribe of the divine. It is said that he knew many of the sacred sciences and taught them to the people. Some of these arts and sciences were astronomy, geometry, mathematics, divine chemistry, human anatomy, and music.

The early church father Clement from Alexandria mentioned in his writings that Hermes Trismegistus was the author of at least 42 books. Among them were books on astronomy and the music of the gods. Hermes Trismegistus is mentioned on the Rosetta Stone.

The German theologian, Albertus Magnus, reported that an ancient tablet written by Hermes Trismegistus was found by Alexander the Great in his conquest of the world. These tablets are known as The Emerald Tablets. The tablets were found in a tomb and were an emerald color.

Depiction of the Emerald Tablet

The tablets were later translated by many scholars including Sir Isaac Newton. Newton's translation made the text of the emerald tablets available in Europe. One of the main themes of the tablets was that things on Earth, are symbolic of things in heaven.

Another writing attributed to Hermes Trismegistus is called The Divine Pymander, which in English is translated "The Divine Shepherd of Man". Justin Martyr and Tertullian are reported to have said that if anyone wanted to know about The Creator of the universe, they should read the writings of Hermes Trismegistus.

Starboard Quest

It is notable, that the early church fathers were quite particular about what outside reading they would be inspired by. They deemed Plato, Aristotle, and Hermes Trismegistus as being ok. In later years some of them changed their minds.

There are many ancient scholars who mentioned Hermes Trismegistus in their writings. The fact that he wrote many interesting books is notable, but there are things far more incredible that are to be discovered about this mysterious person.

Information about him is found all over the ancient world. Legends concerning him surface in several cultures and religions. He was apparently known by varied names in several locations and in a number of different religions.

In the land of Egypt there are rock inscriptions believed to be the oldest writings in the world. These writings are called the pyramid texts. The epigraphs are thousands of years old. Perhaps the most interesting writing is the pictorial hieroglyphic of a man getting taken up into heaven without dying. The imagery is impressive. Where does it come from, and who is the person ascending into heaven?

The answer to this question may be found in the writings of the early church father Lactantius. Lactantius proclaimed Hermes Trismegistus was a prophet. He mentioned that Hermes was imbued with every kind of learning, so that the knowledge of many subjects earned for him the name Trismegistus (meaning the thrice greatest) Lactantius said of Hermes Trismegistus "he was taken from among men and placed with the gods".

The Sumerians long held that before the flood, there lived a powerful king named, Etana who ascended into heaven.

The Babylonians were the dominant record keepers of their day. In their writings they spoke of a man named Utuabzu. The Babylonians said this man was taken up to heaven without seeing death and was never seen again.

The Muslims, who represent a branch of Abrahamic Monotheistic religion, believe in a prophet they called, Idris. They believe that Idris was the founder of numerous sciences. They believe he migrated to Egypt. They say he inscribed certain sciences on two pillars, and then ascended to heaven without dying.

It is notable, that many researchers in numerous cultures spoke of a person ascending into heaven without experiencing death. The person, known by various names, is nearly always mentioned as being knowledgeable about music, astronomy, geometry and other arts and sciences.

Earlier in the book, it was mentioned, that the ascending music scale is symbolic of a cosmological map. The names of the notes correlate to the various levels of the heavens and convey the idea of ascension.

It was also brought out that Pythagoras learned this music scale from Egyptian priests who had, in turn, had the knowledge of music handed down to them from Hermes Trismegistus.

Remember what a music "scale" is, "scale" means a "ladder" and each of the notes in the scale are all Latin names for the different levels of space and the various spiritual levels of heaven.

Who would be a better person to map out the regions of the ascending levels of space than someone who had done it himself?

Who would be a better candidate to map out the human body and show that it is a microcosm of All reality than someone was shown the secrets of human anatomy, the actual universe, and the realms of spiritual beings?

According to ancient writings, both the music scale and the human body are cosmological maps, that show the layout of all visible and invisible reality.

In ancient records of Egypt, there is documentation of a man they called Imhotep. The records say that Imhotep was a prophet, healer, sage, mathematician, architect, artisan, astronomer, and a master of all things. The records say he was given the plans of how to construct the Pyramids in a dream he was given from heaven.

There are several Arabian historians who preserved much of the history of Egypt. Some of the writings are preserved in the British Museum in manuscript 7503.

The great Arab scholar, Masoudi, who passed away in 967 A.D. tells the story of a man named Surid. Surid is reported to have been a king in Egypt before the Pharaohs. Masoudi says of Surid, "Surid, one of the kings of

Egypt before the flood, built the two Great Pyramids. He goes on to say that Surid had a vision of a great catastrophe that was coming, and for this reason he built the pyramids.

Plato wrote in his opening in the book, "Timaeus" that there were two ancient pillars erected. One was made to be imperishable to fire, and the other made to be indestructible by water, both covered in valuable knowledge.

Syncellus was a Byzantine chronicler and ecclesiastic. He had spent many years in Palestine as a monk. He was appointed synkellos to Tarasius, Patriarch of Constantinople. He later retired to a monastery to write a book on world history before he died in 810 A.D. Part of what he recorded is that Hermes Trismegistus erected an upright stone column which contained mysterious knowledge of astronomy.

Cedrenus was a monk and Byzantine historian who wrote a book on the history of the world, sometime around 1050 A.D.. Cedrenus associated Hermes Trismegistus with Enoch. Cedrenus said that Enoch, inscribed the science of astronomy on two pillars, one on stone to resist water, and one on brick to withstand fire.

Historian Titus Flavius Josephus wrote that the sons of Seth recorded and preserved their knowledge of astronomy and other wisdom in stone monuments.

The Jewish historian Josephus, in speaking of the descendants of Seth wrote, "They also were the inventors of a peculiar sort of wisdom which is concerned with the heavenly bodies and their order, and that their inventions might not be lost before they were sufficiently known, upon Adam's prediction that the world was to be destroyed at one time by the force of fire, at another time by the violence and quantity of water, they made two pillars: the one of brick, the other of stone; they inscribed their discoveries upon them both, that in case the pillar of brick should be destroyed by the flood, the pillar of stone would remain, and exhibit these discoveries to mankind; and also inform them that there was another pillar of brick erected by them. Now this remains in the land of Siriad (Egypt) to this day."

The Jewish people don't call the Great Pyramid the same thing as what most modern people do. They call it "the pillar of Enoch". The Hebrew word for "pillar" means, "monumental stone". What they are referring to then, is the monumental stone of Enoch.

The Jews have a book called "The Book of Jubilees". Fragments of this book were found in the Dead Sea Scrolls. In this book is written the following; "He (Enoch) was the first one from among the children of men that are born on the earth to learn writing, and knowledge and wisdom, and he wrote the signs of heaven according to the order of the months in a book (the book of Enoch) he was the first to write a testimony, and he testified to the children of men concerning the future generations of the world".

In other words, what this is implying, is that Enoch was shown the whole prophetic future of the world before it happened. Including the great flood, and the birth, death, resurrection, and ascension of Jesus Christ before it happened. He placed this in a monument of stone. The story of the prophecy went out across the whole world. It probably went out to all people of various backgrounds, who had different names for Christ.

There is a book called, "The Book of Jasher that showed up in 1840. In it, it's claimed that Enoch was a king in Egypt before the reign of the pharaohs.

Among the Dead Sea Scrolls was a book called "The Book of Enoch". The book explains how Enoch was taken by angels and shown all the secrets of creation. He was shown all the secrets of nature. All the secrets of the universe. He was shown the future of planet Earth and all that would take place in the future of the planet. In fact, the large majority of all the Dead Sea scrolls preserved by the Essenes we're about Enoch.

The ancient text, The Divine Pymander, reads, "Hermes (Trismegistus), he understanding all things, who also saw the whole of things together, and having seen, considered them, and having considered them was powerful to explain and show them. For what he committed to characters, concealing the most part, being silent with wisdom, and speaking

Starboard Quest

opportunity, in order that in all the duration of the world thereafter should search out these things; and thus, having ordered the gods, his brethren, to become his escort, he ascended towards the constellations."

Witnesses from cultures all around the world have recorded information of a man who was shown the secrets of the universe, inscribed them into stone monuments, and then ascended into heaven without dying. All of Earth's future is said to have been recorded in the Great Pyramid. Before it was placed in the pyramid, it was written in the stars. The various signs of the zodiac were a picture story which prophesied how things were going to play out on this planet. Most of the future was known before it happened. Certain degrees of understanding about this spread across the world. In time, much of the knowledge was lost. People within cultures only had fragments of prophecies. These were handed down verbally in most nations throughout the generations.

This is most likely why you can go to nearly any culture or religion on the face of the Earth, and they all have similar stories. They all have stories of a worldwide flood. They all have information of a Messiah who would come and go through death, burial, resurrection, and ascension. It all comes from a previous understanding and a detailed pre-knowledge, a prophecy, so to speak, of what was scheduled to happen on planet Earth.

There are many religions that claim that a virgin conceived and gave birth to the Son of God. Some of these religions were around for a long time before Christianity. This has led to some people claiming that Christianity just borrowed stories from earlier religions.

All these claims of similar stories from various religions don't disprove Christianity, they actually authenticate it. All these similar stories show, is that there was a previous knowledge of what was going to happen, and it was dispersed throughout the entire world at one time. Another thing to consider, is that many times throughout history, saints were confused with gods. When Enoch came and built the Great Pyramid, people were amazed. Later generations made a god out of him. Various scholars have pointed out the similarities between the Egyptian god, Thoth the god of writing, and Enoch who was known as the great scribe. They claim that Thoth was just a god the Egyptians invented based on Enoch because they were so amazed by him and what was accomplished through him. Also, the Greeks made Enoch Hermes and the Romans Mercury. This has happened all the time throughout history, it's called Saint worship.

So, basically, you have many scholars from various religions, all basically saying the same types of things. They all say a man came to this Earth, was shown the secrets of the Earth and universe, inscribed them into stone monuments and then left this earth without dying. Isn't it quite ironic then, that as scholars study the Great Pyramid of Egypt, they conclude that it's a great astronomical marker and calendar? They examine it and are baffled. The pyramid shows the distance of the earth to the sun. It demonstrates the weight and width of the Earth. It sets on the exact center of the earth mass. Its inner chambers appear to be a calendar which marks out the most notable events that have taken place in Earth's history. There are so many measurements in the Great Pyramid that directly correlate to the layout of the universe, that it would take volumes of books to write them all down.

The astronomical information exhibited by the pyramid seems endless. Modern scholars research it and can't figure out how ancient people knew so much about astronomy.

The great astronomer Nikolas Copernicus implied that as he made his astronomical discoveries, he was amazed to find out that Hermes Trismegistus had already written about these astronomical findings thousands of years before.

Let's go back to teachings of Pythagoras for just a moment. Remember, he is the one who is credited with introducing the music scale to the world. There is a special way of tuning a musical instrument called Pythagorean tuning. This involves tuning the A- note of the music scale to 432 hertz. Where did he get the idea to tune instruments in this way? In addition, ancient instruments found in ancient cultures are found to be tuned to the 432 hertz tuning.

If we look at some of the measurements of the Pyramids in Egypt and other places in the world, we find something amazing regarding the number 432.

The pyramid Menkaure in Egypt is 345.6 feet tall, which is a multiple of 432. (432x8=345.6) and is 216 wide at the base. (432 divided by 2.)

The Khafre pyramid is 216 meters wide at the base (216x2=432) and 144 meters high (144x3=432.

The Khufu pyramid has a base to height ratio of 7/11. The base of the pyramid is 432 long cubits wide at its base. If you take 432 and multiply it by the 7/11 base to height ratio, you get 275 which is how many long cubits high the pyramid is.

The number 432 is found in the pyramid of the sun in Teotihuacan as well. The base is 432 cubits, and its height is 216 cubits (216x2=432).

There are many more measurements in the pyramids that are multiples of 432. They are too numerous to mention.

All the vibrations of the Pythagorean music scales are multiples of 432.

It is said that the Sethites encoded divine secrets into the architectural alignments inside and outside of the Great Pyramid, the sphinx, and huge temples.

The Greek historian Herodotus of Halicarnassus went to Egypt as early as 440 B.C.

He reports that at that time, the Great Pyramid was covered with polished white casing stones. Not only that, but the outside of the pyramid was covered with writings of sacred texts. Herodotus is also known as Al-Masudi, or Masoudi. Whether the pyramid was covered in writings, is not presently understood by the common man.

Masoudi's historic manuscript is preserved in the British Museum as Document 9575. In the document he says that the faces of the Great Pyramid were inscribed with unknown and indecipherable writings of a forgotten time.

Ebn Haukal, another Arab Historian recorded that the surface of the Two largest Pyramids were covered with inscriptions from top to bottom. Small inscriptions all over the four faces of the Great Pyramid would constitute the most incredible, extensive, and comprehensive library in the world. If this were true, it would have been the largest book on the planet.

It has yet to be proven there was writing on it. It is notable, however that early Arabs and Greeks recorded that the ancient script on the Great Pyramid was still observable in their era. The writings were barely visible, almost erased by the ravages of time.

In 1356 A.D. an earthquake struck the Muslim city of Cairo near Giza. Over a period of several decades the Muslims stripped the casing stones off the Great Pyramid to rebuild Cairo. Some of the mosques built from the stolen stone are still standing.

For centuries, it was only a rumor that the Great Pyramid was covered with white casing stones. It hadn't been proven. Then in 1837 Col. Vyse found casing stones still attached to the Great Pyramid at its base under a pile of rubble. By that time, any writing that may have been on the casing stones was worn off.

One may wonder, if there were indeed writings on the surface of the Great Pyramid, what did they say?

It is believed by some researchers, that Divine, celestial, and terrestrial histories, secrets, prophecies, and angelic mysteries were inscribed onto the pyramid. Perhaps some of the ancient texts mentioned earlier, such as the Book of Enoch.

When you stop and think of it, what an ingenious way to preserve all the sacred writings, geometry, astronomy, math, history of the world, and other sacred knowledge from a worldwide catastrophe. Inscribe all the sacred knowledge onto a huge monument. Then later, scribes could just come and write it down.

The idea to encode geometrical and astronomical knowledge in the measurements of its geometry, and write the future history within its inner chambers was divine genius. If there were actual writings on the surface of the pyramid, there is no scientific proof of it. One must admit though, it is a very interesting idea.

Some researchers have gone as far as to say that when Moses wrote the account of creation, currently found in the Book of Genesis, he wrote down the text directly off the Great pyramid. The surface texts were said to contain the entire history of what had gone on in heaven, which would include records of the angelic wars. It would have also chronicled what had happened on planet Earth in its history, and the future histories of all that would happen.

Starboard Quest

The stars and its constellations were the first place that the whole saga of Earths future history was written. It was written again in the Great Pyramid, which has a direct connection to the zodiac signs. The pyramid is like a temple of talking stones, which speaks to us the secrets of the history of the world.

There is an old text called "The Apocalypse of Matthias the Scribe" In the text, Matthias The Scribe describes being taken to a white mountain, with four perfect sides, and the capstone of the mountain is missing. In chapter 4: 7-10 he says the following.

"Then did I continue my search of the mountain, and lo, I perceived the appearance of words of an unknown kind upon the face of the stones.

There were thousands upon thousands and countless many stones. And on them all were written words of mystery.

As I watched, my vision became altered and, in the spirit, I beheld the formation of newer words. I was perplexed, for this writing I knew was one of songs uttered not by human tongues.

Words became merged with other words and symbols. Though their meanings were not made known to me, by wisdom of the Spirit did I know that these were songs of power."

Where this ancient text came from, and if this was a real vision someone had, we don't know now. The thing being noted here, is the idea of the songs of angels being inscribed into the pyramid. Where did this idea come from?

Clement from Alexandria said that he witnessed the books of Hermes. One of the books was a music book.

If indeed, the writings of Hermes Trismegistus were inscribed upon the Great Pyramid, and did get copied down directly off of the pyramid, then it would make sense that one of his rumored books was called, "The hymns of the gods". The vision of Matthias the scribe would make more sense then. In his vision, he said there were songs written on the surface of the Great Pyramid, which were not sung by human tongues.

It's time to move on to the next message in a bottle.

"In that day shall there be an altar to the Lord in the midst of the land of Egypt, and a pillar at the border thereof to the Lord."
Isaiah 19:19

The Greeks

For centuries, people have marveled at the genius of the Greek philosophers. It has been said that the pillars of modern society were put into place by these men. Did they dream up all the knowledge of these various areas of learning on their own, or did they have help we don't know about?

Researchers are amazed by the fabulous contributions of the Greeks in the areas of architecture, government, philosophy, astronomy, music, chemistry, and the other arts and sciences that these men were involved with. The Greek philosophers are said to have been the originators of our whole modern way of life.

It may be true that it seems as if the Greek philosophers built the foundations of modern society in various categories of society. As a result of this, the force they have been in the preservation of mankind has been staggering. However, one thing is very often overlooked.

Many people don't know that many Greek philosophers such as Hippocrates, Pythagoras, Socrates, Plato and others traveled to Egypt to expand their knowledge. This is a known fact mentioned in historic writings.

They studied in Egypt. Some of them are said to have studied in the vast library of Alexandria. The library contained secret knowledge of many of the different arts and sciences. Some of the knowledge at the library was said to have been garnered from the books of Hermes Trismegistus.

Pythagoras was known to have lived in Egypt for 34 years. Plato was in Egypt for 15 years. There were others in Egypt as well, such as, Thales of Miletus, Solon, And Orpheus.

Pythagoras is said to have studied under the Egyptian Priests and to have been initiated into the secrets of Egypt. In addition, some researchers say that Plato was initiated into the mysteries after going through a secret door into the Great Pyramid.

Remember what Josephus and other historians said regarding the preservation of ancient arts and sciences? He said that the Sons of Seth came and inscribed astronomical knowledge into pillars (the word "pillar" translates into "stone monuments" in Hebrew) They did it, so that the knowledge received would be passed on to humanity in other ages. It was done to help humanity. It was done to help preserve people through maintaining helpful knowledge.

The Greeks went to Egypt, obtained knowledge, and then went back to Greece and implemented their findings. The success they achieved in their society in turn became the blueprint for successful societies around the entire world, then, to a certain extent, was not the plan to preserve knowledge for succeeding generations successful? When the founding fathers of the United States set up the government, they patterned it after the government of Greece. The Greeks learned from the Egyptians.

Can we even calculate how many human lives have been spared, and how much suffering has been eliminated from humanity, by having well-ordered societies all over the world? Do we not owe credit to Greek philosophers for putting these things in order? In turn, can we not trace back the origins of many of these ideas to ancient Egypt?

The Greeks are recognized for having contributed many positive things to the modern world. For the sake of time and simplicity, let's just look at a couple of areas, and see how they may have had their roots in Egyptian concepts.

Starboard Quest

The Greeks are known for their fabulous architecture. When they built buildings, they built them according to the laws of sacred geometry. Their buildings are known for being built with harmonic principles. The golden proportion and the golden spiral are found in their buildings. In fact, their buildings have been called "frozen music". This is most likely because musical proportions can be found within their mathematical proportions.

This picture is an example of classic Greek architecture.

Greek structures were built nearly mathematically perfect. This is a well-known fact. The question, that modern researchers don't seem to be asking is; where did they get the idea to build their structures in this way?

Very simply, could not their idea to build things on Earth according to the laws of sacred geometry have descended from Egypt?

The Great Pyramid preceded any architecture in Greece. The pyramid was constructed using sacred geometry and is aligned with astronomical events. Could not the Greeks have learned from these structures and other structures in their many years studying in Egypt and then brought the building plans for these types of structures back to Greece? Isn't it highly likely that they did? If so, then the building principals used in the Great Pyramid have continued to bless the world with sound buildings to this day.

Another example of something positive the Greeks have contributed to the modern world is their high standards for music. In fact, Socrates was quoted as saying that to achieve a utopian society you'd first have to purge it of its toxic music. They were firm believers in getting music right in their society. The Chinese were this way as well.

The Greeks had seven different music modes, all connected with music notes and planets and constellations. You would play in specific modes, to produce determined effects in the listener. This has been gone over more fully earlier in the book.

The question again rises, where did they come up with this idea? They had legends of gods playing music. They had 9 different muses who were spirits inspiring musicians.

If you study Hebrew writings, you will find that musical super beings called angels sing. During the renaissance period they classified angels in 9 different categories. The book of Enoch gives an account of the singing of angels.

The highly advanced societies of Egypt and Greece placed a high value on theology, music, Astronomy, and the various arts. Society flourished and the light of wisdom shown across the Earth. However, a dark chapter in human history was looming on the horizon.

What this event was, and the period that followed it, are found in the next clue which is heading towards the ship right now.

The Renaissance

As the next message in a bottle is opened, it's discovered that a small turquoise stone accompanies the scroll. As the scroll is rolled open and observed, this is how it reads,

"Earthly libraries may vanish, but the inner library will always await you."

It has been said that knowledge is power. Throughout the centuries, one of the best ways for societies to keep their citizens on the path of understanding has been through their libraries. One of the greatest libraries the world has ever known was the library at Alexandria in Egypt.

According to Wikipedia historic records, the library was accidentally destroyed in a fire set by the soldiers of Julius Caesar in 48 B.C. Over the years, more vandals and armies attacked it. Finally, there was a lack of interest in it, and it dwindled away. Today there is no trace of the library. This was a dark hour in the literary history of the world.

Apparently, not all the books were lost, it is thought that some of the information was taken and stored in other places. However, within a couple of hundred years, the world had slipped into a deep ignorance which lasted from about 400 A.D. to 1,000 A.D. then a time for change came.

In 1517, the reformation began and lasted about 31 years. Due to the freedom brought by the reformation, People who had once been restricted by the Catholic Church began to be more independent thinkers.

Aspects of the renaissance had already begun prior to the reformation, but with the effects of the reformation coming into play over extended periods of time, the arts and sciences began to really flourish. Martin Luther was a song writer who said that every kind of modern instrument should be used. Music flourished.

During, the reformation, and then for a couple of hundred years after it, an age of science and exploration set in. Old Greek texts were rediscovered. Sir Isaac Newton translated the Emerald Tablets. Hermetic literature from ancient Egypt began spreading. Johannes Kepler was born and at one point in his life, began reintroducing the idea of the music of the spheres. Within 200 years of the reformation, Bach, Beethoven, and Mozart were born. For creative energies to come into expression, an atmosphere had to be created for it to come forth in.

What may sometimes be overlooked about the Renaissance period, is that part of what happened during that time, is that much of the forgotten ancient wisdom from Egypt, Greece, and other ancient cultures was rediscovered. People began delving into various ancient texts and sciences.

It was during this time, that the science of chemistry really took hold. The practice had originated way back in Egypt, but a widespread interest in it returned.

Many of the medicines we have today were discovered by chemists over the centuries.

This was at least in part, due to the alchemists. The alchemists believed that there were secrets locked away in matter that could be unlocked. Many of the alchemists were highly religious and believed that they had a divine mission to discover the secrets of creation hidden in matter. Some believed that were on a holy mission to unveil the enigmas.

Eventually, people of all walks of life and religions began to believe they could transform base metals into gold.

In some cases, they claimed to have accomplished the feat. Some just did it out of greed, while others believed they could help society if they had enough wealth.

Eventually, a paranoia set in. Governments began to worry that if the common man learned how to manufacture gold, it would bankrupt entire nations. Also, alchemists who were greedy, gave the whole science a bad name.

Alchemy was against the law. What psychological trick could be played upon the people to get them to stop delving in this? Well, one good way is to try to convince religious people that chemistry was evil. Soon tales began to circulate about witches conjuring up evil potions.

Sure, there was a misuse of this science by some, but this was not the original intent of the practice. Certain people dirtied the name of the art.

This isn't how chemistry started. There were many religious people who believed it was their religious duty to unlock the healing remedies and secrets of nature to help mankind. They did this by studying chemistry.

Many people from all kinds of backgrounds and religions set out to discover the secret of transforming base metals into gold. In the process, they discovered hundreds of compounds and medicines that are useful to us today.

Paracelsus was a physician, alchemist, lay theologian, and philosopher of the German Renaissance

Devout Protestant Sir Isaac Newton studied alchemy secretly for 50 years. In his lifetime, the practice of it was still punishable by death at the hands of the Government.

In the modern day, there are several groups who like to claim ownership of alchemy and people like Hermes Trismegistus, Sir Isaac Newton, Paracelsus, and many others. Nothing could be further from the truth.

Many the alchemists were Christian people, many who were Protestants. Paracelsus was a Bible salesman who had memorized the whole

Bible by heart. He was called the Martin Luther of medicine. He found many cures in an unconventional way. He was a master alchemist. Yet, there are many Religious and non-religious groups in the modern day who would like to claim him, and the practice of chemistry as a science of their own. For example, after Paracelsus died (some said he was murdered) works appeared which claimed they were by him, which were forgeries and depicted him as a sorcerer. This was a man who was very outspoken against the Catholic Church, but at the same time he was very knowledgeable about the Scriptures.

In time, a belief in the elixir of life set in. It was a supposed formula that would grant immortality to whoever drank it. Rumors circulated that there were some who had found the secret of how to make the formula.

Alchemy originated in ancient Egypt. It comes from two words which mean "divine chemistry." What is very interesting about alchemy, is that there are some who claim that Hermes Trismegistus was the founder of this science. Sir Francis Bacon openly stated that Hermes Trismegistus and Enoch were the exact same person.

People study history, but in so doing, there are obvious questions that are never asked. When you see the mass obsession that there was with alchemy in certain times of history, and the claims that there was an elixir of life which would grant immortality, it should create the question; what was the basis of this belief? What evidence did they have that such an accomplishment was even remotely possible? Where did they come up with the idea in the first place? How could they have dreamed up such a practice? Where did the belief that a human being could be living on this Earth and become immortal come from in the first place?

My guess would be, that it stems from the belief that a man walked out of this world without dying. A man, whom, according to Jewish, Egyptian, Babylonian, and Arabian historians had inscribed sacred knowledge into the Great Pyramid. A man whom according to various hermetic literature is said to have been highly knowledgeable about chemistry. Some ancient texts say the place he was taken up into heaven, was from the center of the Earth, right where the pyramids stand. We've been told our whole lives the Great Pyramid is a monument commemorating immortality. It's not very often that we ask ourselves the question; Why would they have built a monument commemorating immortality? Someone must have thought something quite significant, and notable had happened there, in order for them to be willing to take huge stones across vast expanses in order to construct the monument.

So, in a science such as chemistry, is it possible that there are other areas that it's principals would work, other than by mixing chemicals?

It is possible that this science could be carried over into music. It is interesting, that music has transformative properties. As has been mentioned, sound vibrations can shape matter through a cymatics instrument. A certain sound vibration can be passed through water to cause light to come forth out of water in a process called, "sonoluminescence".

Is there something sound can accomplish that we are not all that familiar with? The very names of the notes in a scale hint of ascension. Is it more of an agent of transformation than what we thought? Some researchers believe that the Great Pyramid was an acoustic device. Others claim there is a special energy in the pyramids that keeps fruit fresh longer and sharpens dull razor blades.

Even on a personal human level, music has a power to transform. To begin with, it is highly interesting how a person's feelings can be transformed by music. A person can feel sad, and after listening to a happy song they can suddenly feel happy. Music has been proven to increase the levels of dopamine in the human body.

Music can boost memory, build task endurance, lighten your mood, reduce anxiety, and stave off depression. There are many things it can do. A more in-depth study should be done on it. Perhaps the study should begin by asking ourselves how music has the power to do this. What is this invisible substance called, "music"?

There is a deep musical knowledge buried within humanity. For that treasure to come forth, conditions must be just right. Things have been falling into place over long extended periods of time. In the divine musical chemistry of the ages, all the ingredients must be poured forth into the world. It seems as if we are really close to something new, something extraordinary that is about to take place in the musical chemistry of the ages.

The next message in a bottle drifts our way. It's the next clue in our treasure hunt to discover the musical secrets of the epochs.

Beyond the
Flawed Power Structure

The next bottle is opened. The message reads,

"That which is, is a steppingstone to a higher musical realm."

There is a gypsum stone in the bottle.

Martin Luther, in the statue above, said music needed to be reclaimed and refined from people with perverted minds. The word "refined" means to remove impurities or unwanted elements from a substance.

Music, although invisible, is indeed a substance. It's a substance in a similar way that electricity is a substance, invisible, but real, nonetheless.

Throughout history, we see various scholars discussing music, and how to best implement it in their societies. The Greeks had very strict rules they placed upon the music of their society. The Chinese also had very disciplined concept of music and even put a great importance on what tuning music was played in. This type of thinking has just about disappeared entirely in the modern day.

Although some of the musicians of the past did have questionable antics and behaviors that were less than virtuous. It still seems like the music itself was still held to higher standards.

It is true that not all early music masters were always paragons of virtue. Pythagoras is rumored to have had a student thrown overboard off a ship for disagreeing with him. The student had supposedly come up with a mathematical equation that proved some of Pythagoras's theories wrong.

Another great songwriter, who was learned in all the wisdom of the Egyptians was Moses. He once got so mad he accidentally beat a man to death and had to flee the country. Yet the song he wrote was divine.

A person can investigate the music masters of the past and find they had human flaws and errors. At the same time, it seems that they were always trying to bring musical flawlessness to greater heights of perfection.

Composers like John Sebastian Bach and Ludwig Von Beethoven put tremendous thought into their compositions. They played all their pieces in Pythagorean tuning. Many of their compositions were of a serious nature.

John Sebastian Bach

As far as being of a serious mindset, composers like Martin Luther, John and Charles Wesley, and others were excellent.

In this current time, there are a few composers who hold to the seriousness of the musical masters from the past. However, a large percentage of what is played on major radio stations in the modern day, seems to be just the opposite.

Ludwig Van Beethoven

A lot of it has foolish lyrics of no meaning or lasting value. It's played in a less perfect tuning than what was once used. It appears as if they think they can hide their lack of talent by playing music so loud it hurts people's ears. Intelligent people see what they're doing though.

They play backbeats and use distorted instruments. They promote a lack of morals. They do this, while all the time sporting egos. They

John Wesley

appear to have very little integrity or character and it seems like they are worshipped by people who are a lot like them in those regards. To each his own. Who knows what's in their hearts? The hope would be that they would be forgiven and be inspired to do something better.

Think of what a contrast they are to the humble men of old who sought out perfection within their music. Sure, the masters made mistakes too, but they had a vision. To err is human.

What is the purpose then, of the thousands of musicians who have appeared on the Earth to work a dark alchemy on the masses?

It's not just prominent people in the industry that are causing the problem. It's musicians from every level of society. It's musicians operating everywhere from bar rooms to large concert halls, to small gatherings, to churches. It's not as if no good is coming through what's being played, it's just that everything needs to take a step up. Some corrections need to take place.

Almost all of them play distorted instruments, backbeats, and use non-Pythagorean tunings, and etc. They are at war with the music of the spheres, and most of them don't know it. If everything about what they are doing was wrong, it would be no challenge to rise above it. They must have a certain degree of good in what they are doing, that the greater good can be made manifest.

The modern music system is a structure that has been allowed to exist in order that it can be transcended. For a greater musical perfection to arise, there has to be an existing structure of an inferior nature already in place. It is there to be risen above. Things were never intended to stay at this level forever. Things are made to be continually expanding and rising higher.

The idea of transcendence is shown plainly in the music scale itself. You rise note by note, until you reach the, what? The new octave. Once you reach the new octave, the old musical scale you were just in, is done away with.

Why are there questionable people, drug pushers, criminals, and people of I'll repute making music? Why have they been given such prominent places of power in the world? Why has the sacred science of music been profaned?

They're setting the stage for the light. They were given gifts and allotments of power to be allowed to create an atmosphere of darkness so that the light could arise above it in an ultimate victory over darkness.

It's as Shakespeare once wrote, "All the world is a stage and all the Men and Women merely players." Some people are content with playing the part of musical villains. They were necessary in the play.

If they weren't doing what they're doing, it wouldn't be possible to bring something greater into manifestation. They don't know that this is the purpose they serve, or they would stop doing what they are doing.

There is a higher octave coming. It's a higher level. It's a new music scale. It's time to climb up into that new scale. The curtain is about to be drawn open on the final act.

As we continue, in our journey across the sound waves, another message awaits us just ahead.

The New Octave

Now comes the final message in our musical treasure hunt; in the bottle, there is a diamond, which is a white stone. The scroll simply reads,

"Rise into the new octave."

On our journey, we have learned that the music scale can be likened unto a brilliant, resplendent, and dazzling musical ladder which ascends through the various levels of the heavens. Each ascending note on the music scale can be likened to each ascending rung on a ladder as it heads towards the high-pitched apex.

Pythagoras spoke of a clandestine place called "the blessed eighth sphere". The blessed eighth sphere was simply a place beyond our solar system where celestial beings were thought to dwell. There they sang their songs and made music. There, in the place beyond the highest rung on the ladder.

Each of the 7 orbs of our solar system, visible to the naked eye, were likened to the seven notes of a music scale. Each note, or harmony had a power which was beneficial, yet restrictive.

In ancient man's way of thinking, even though the physical universe exhibits beauty and harmony, being restricted by the exerted powers of the planets is a limitation.

The ancient thought was that there are octaves above the music of the spheres. Even though the music of the spheres is excellent, there's something even more excellent. The idea was, that there are certain people who were born to rise to those higher enthralling octaves which reached beyond the music of the spheres.

It was thought that once a soul ascended beyond that 7th level, and into the 8th sphere, it had reached a new octave. This was a luminescent place beyond the music of man, beyond the music of the spheres, and into the musical empires of the angels.

Perhaps a good place to start in our lifelong musical education, is to begin in a humble manner by at least trying to improve the music of man, by patterning it to certain elements of the music of the spheres and its divine mathematics.

As noble of an undertaking as that may be, there are still levels far beyond the music of the spheres. In fact, the planets and universes are just symbols to show man what is within the inner being. The true ascension is within, in simplicity. The vast structures of the universe, and the complex studies of man, only give a small glimpse into the greatness of inner space.

Perhaps as those who are destined to excel and grow into the understanding of a deeper internal music do so, songs will dawn within their consciousness which resemble the songs which existed before the sun, moon, and stars.

Music, by its very nature is pointing out, the idea of transcendence. The octave, itself is a miracle. Two notes that become one, by ascending all the way up the scale.

Music as it is known in this world, and even as it is written on paper is limited. The music staff itself is a microcosm of time and space. The notes represent time, and the spaces between the lines on the music staff, represent space. There is a place beyond time and space.

There is a marking in musical notation which is placed up above the lines of a music staff. It is an octiva. It takes the shape of the numeral 8. This means, play all the notes on the sheet music, one octave up from what they are written on the sheet.

Perhaps that musical notation can serve an even greater symbolic purpose. That purpose being, to show us that there is a music beyond this world's music. We are playing off the sheet music of this life of time and space. However, when we see the marking of the new octave, it's time to play the music at a whole higher octave.

Let that new higher octave lead to that particular timeless music, beyond all Earthly music, that we can see humble men and women being elevated into as we gaze into the looking glass of yesteryear.

There is a music beyond man, and a music beyond the universe. There is even a music beyond the angels. This is a music of the One who spoke creation into existence.

In the endless never-never lands of light. Arise the spellbinding epiphanies of everlasting sounds. It is there, that musical oracles whisper through the ghostly utopias of infinity.

The incandescent sounds, divine and exacting, shimmer like jewels at the apex and zenith of the golden ladder.

The reflection of that ladder shines on the glassy sea of the ethereal harbor. There the ship comes to rest, surrounded by the seraphic and transcendental treasures of timeless sound.

Conclusion

A time of great world change is set just before us. We patiently await the inevitable return of the great symphonic beyond. The symphony illuminates us and becomes a medium for the upper light, which shines its phosphorus rays through the deep forests of musical night.

There has been a universal hope throughout the ages. The hope is connected to a secret knowledge from Earth's childhood. Man has sought to activate a beautiful musical chemistry. Human beings have forged forward in divine expectation, desiring to unlock the secret, ancient song of eternity. It is a song which has been sealed away from man for ages, and has only faintly and distantly been heard in the whispers of the music of the spheres.

Ancient wise men and scribes believed that an ascending soul, like an ascending note on a musical scale, would eventually arrive at the threshold of the doorway which led to the place of the glorious liberty of all things. It was likened to a note which had reached the new octave.

The threshold was found near the top rung of a celestial ladder. Through stepping up and into what Pythagoras called, "The blessed eighth sphere" they would climb up beyond the world of men and into the region of songs in the great beyond. Although these men had lofty ideas, they can easily be pictured as being humble men of humility and simplicity. They were doing the best they could.

After thousands of years it would be very difficult to scientifically prove who these ideas originally came from. However, there's nothing wrong with examining the thoughts of those who came before us. You'll have to decide for yourself what to take and leave out of what they left behind for us. The answers to some of these questions are discovered in the journey you take to the depths of your own inner world.

From the days of Earth's youth there has been a song that has burned in the hearts of men. A longing to get back to that place they feel they came from. Someplace better. There is a right way and a wrong way to ascend, a person has to try to climb the right way and through the right means.

We can not always authenticate some of the non Biblical texts that are said to have come from these people.

Is there not at least something to be learned from the hopes, dreams, and optimism of all those who preceded us whose hearts cried out for something deeper and better? Could this not at least in part, be compared to the notes of the ascending music scale which are always climbing towards something higher? Ironically, at the same time, this ascension is accomplished through becoming more humble. Music has been like a good friend that has walked along side of the human race for thousands of years, admonishing and encouraging them.

There are many other encouragements along the way. One of them is the Great Pyramid. One of the unspoken messages of the Great Pyramid seems to be, "Look up!" It always comes across as if it was intended to point us upward. The structure sets colossal like, on the very center of the Earth, and is a a commemorative monument to ascension and immortality. It used to be covered in white polished stone.

Throughout history, commemorative monuments are set up at places where extraordinary things have taken place. Ask yourself this question; What event took place in Earth's history that has merited being designated by the most incredible monument ever constructed in the history of the world? Could it have something to do with the old writing which states that Enoch was taken up into heaven from near a white mountain at the center of the Earth? Could the pyramid commemorate this event?

In another place in Egypt, in a place away from the Great Pyramid are found what are called "the pyramid texts". The pyramid texts are the oldest texts in the world. Written upon them was found a phrase. The phrase seems to be a message that stretches from dateless past to unending future. Here's what was written, by an unknown person.

"A stairway to the sky is set for me that I may ascend into the sky."

Could it be, that the sky being spoken of, was the sky within? The Great Pyramid, has an ascending passageway within, could that be the stairway? We as humans, are also said to have an inner ascending passageway.

Scattered across many cultures are texts which speak of divine ladders which span from Earth to heaven. Historians can trace ideas of this ladder all the way back to the Great Pyramid. The pyramid itself has a narrow inner upward pathway that leads to the King's chamber. It's interesting symbolism, but what is really behind this symbolism?

A ladder is a narrow pathway that only one can travel at a time. It is a straight and narrow pathway that leads upward. Remember also, that the music scale is a musical ladder with musical notes ascending and descending upon it. Where did this idea come from? How did ancient philosophers know to identify these levels of the music staff, with levels of the heavens? How did they come to an idea that it was a ladder with music ascending and descending upon it?

In the ancient scriptures is the account of Jacob's ladder. In the dream, Jacob seen heaven opened and those who are generally known to be musical beings (angels) ascending and descending upon the ladder.

Finally, and most importantly are the words from one who is above all seers, wisemen, and scribes. One who stands above all arts and sciences. There are those who claim Jesus Christ identified Jacob's ladder. This is what he said, "Truly, truly, I say to you, you will see heaven opened, and the angels of God ascending and descending on the Son of Man."

There are those who say The Lord Jesus Christ identified himself as Jacob's ladder, that the angels were ascending and descending upon. The narrow path, the bridge between earth and heaven. Is the ladder spoken of as Jacob's ladder connected with idea of the ladder that sages in other cultures spoke of? What do you think?

If so, could it be that this is the ultimate treasure that has been sought for throughout the ages. Philosophers and scribes searched and came up with the best illustrations for it they could. Over the centuries some of it may have gotten mixed in with paganism, yet there is a common thread that runs through the whole thing. You don't have to travel to outer space to climb that ladder. All of those symbols out there in the heavens are emblems of the path within. It's a humble ascension.

From chapter to chapter in this book, bottle after bottle of thought has been poured into your mind. I hope that it works a divine musical chemistry in you over extended periods of time and leads you to a wonderful and timeless place. I hope you obtain the higher worlds, while on your journey to the depths of your inner cosmos.

I hope that far beyond the reading of this book, you keep finding and receiving more messages left for you.

Can you, in your minds eye see that message just over yonder, shining on the distant horizon?

Seek the treasures which are from above.

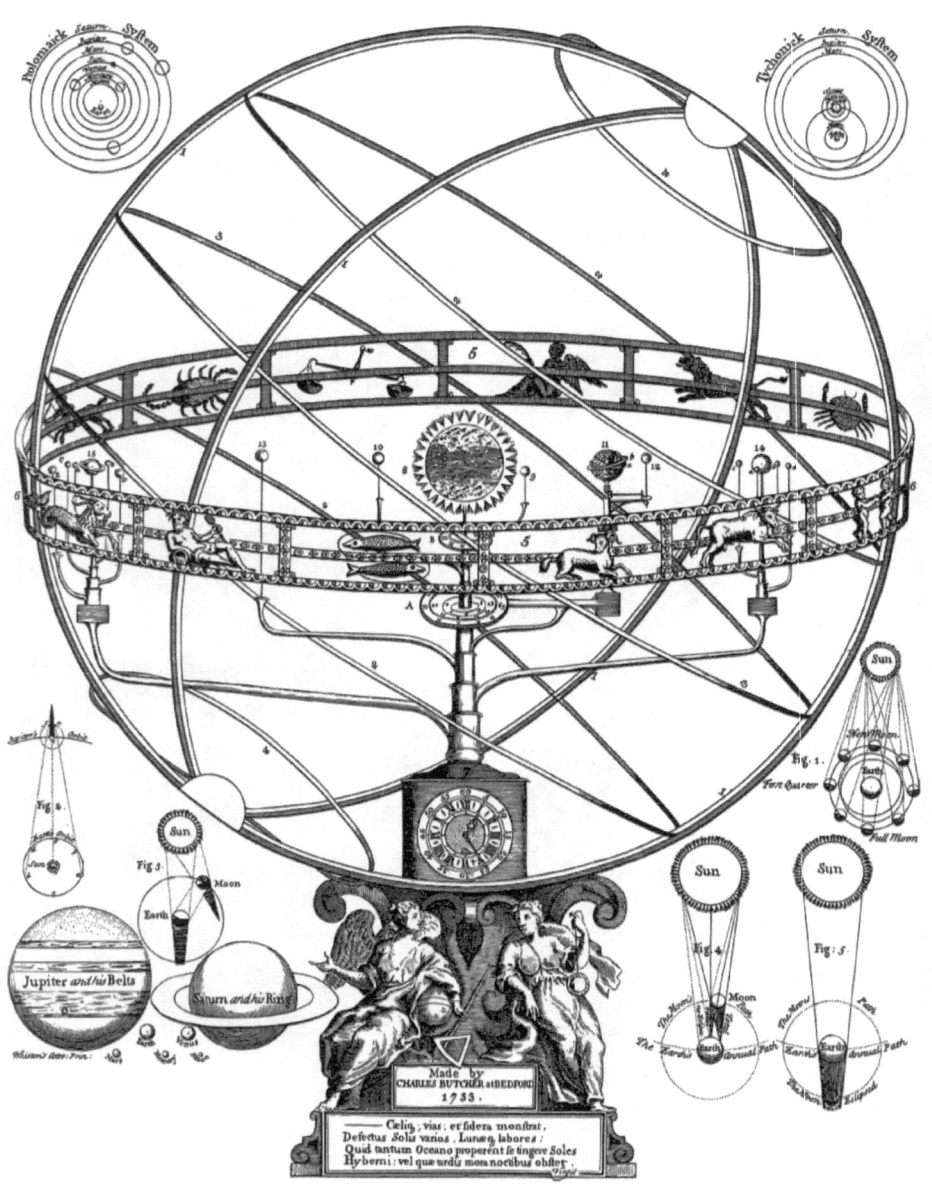

Bibliography

Joscelyn Godwin, Harmonies of Heaven and Earth, Inner Traditions National Rochester, Vermont 1995

David Ellington, The Ancient Language of Sacred Sound, Inner Traditions Vermont 2021

Armin Huseman, The Harmony Of The Human Body, Floris Books 1994

Jonathan Goldman, Healing Sounds, Healing Arts Press 1992

Johannes Kepler, The Harmonies of the World

Manly P Hall, various lectures

Jamie James, The Music of The Spheres Copernicus, New York 1993

John Chambers, The Metaphysical World of Isaac Newton, Destiny Books 2018

Tobias Churton, The Lost Pillars of Enoch, Inner Traditions Vermont 2021

David Tame, The Secret Power Of Music, Destiny Books Vermont 1984

G.R.S. Mead, Hymns of Hermes, Red Wheel /Weissr ME. 1991

Jason M. Breshears ,The Lost Scriptures of Giza, The Book Tree San Diego California 2006

Joscelyn Godwin, The Harmony of The Spheres, Inner Traditions International 1993

Fabre d' Olivet, The Secret Lore of Music, Inner Traditions Vermont 1987

There is more to explore!

Visit starboardquest.com

Follow on Facebook

Make sure you read,

"Starboard Quest, Sailing The Sea Of Sound To Explore Music's Connection To The Universe" and listen to its soundtrack

Listen on YouTube

"In a nutshell, perhaps the simplest explanation for the Starboard Quest concept is that it is a musical message in a bottle for the future."
-THE BOSTON HERALD-

"Music which compels people to gaze inward, introspect, and make a positive change within their lives."
-Minnesota Public Radio-

"Based on mathematics, set patterns, designs, and musical theory, this form of music is deeply entwined with information that is connected with astronomy, geometry, history, and mathematics."
- U.S. and Canada Report-

"Music that breaks free from the norms set in stone in society."
-Universal News Report-

As heard on;

National Public Radio- United States *Radio Disney*
BBC Radio- Europe *Billboard*
Sirius Satellite Radio *Candid Radio*

AND MORE!

www.ingramcontent.com/pod-product-compliance
Lightning Source LLC
Chambersburg PA
CBHW030512130626
46549CB00007B/2964